First Facts®

Whales and Dolphins Up Close

BOTTLENOSE DOLPHINS UP CLOSE

by Jody Sullivan Rake

Consultant:
Deborah Nuzzolo
Education Manager
SeaWorld, San Diego

Capstone
press®

Mankato, Minnesota

First Facts is published by Capstone Press,
151 Good Counsel Drive, P.O. Box 669, Mankato, Minnesota 56002.
www.capstonepress.com

Library of Congress Cataloging-in-Publication Data
Rake, Jody Sullivan.
    Bottlenose dolphins up close / by Jody Sullivan Rake.
    p. cm. — (First facts. Whales and dolphins up close)
    Includes bibliographical references and index.
    Summary: "Presents an up-close look at bottlenose dolphins, including their body
features, habitat, and life cycle" — Provided by publisher.
    ISBN-13: 978-1-4296-2264-6 (hardcover)
    ISBN-10: 1-4296-2264-4 (hardcover)
    1. Bottlenose dolphin — Juvenile literature. I. Title.
QL737.C432R35 2009
599.53'3 — dc22
                                                        2008030103

Editorial Credits
Christine Peterson, editor; Renée T. Doyle, designer; Wanda Winch, photo researcher

Photo Credits
fotolia/Judy, 9 (bottom right)
Getty Images Inc./The Image Bank/Costeau Society, 6
Jeff Rotman, 17
marinethemes.com/Kelvin Aitken, 14 (inset)
Minden Pictures/Flip Nicklin, 8–9, 18; Norbert Wu, 13, 20
Nature Picture Library/Doug Perrine, 14
Seapics.com/Ingrid Visser, 21
Shutterstock/Darryl Vest, 11; Kristian Sekulic, 1, 6 (inset), 13 (inset), cover;
    Lyndsey McCall, 19; Marilyn Volan, background throughout; Timmary, splash
    element throughout
SuperStock, Inc./age fotostock, 5

1 2 3 4 5 6 14 13 12 11 10 09

TABLE OF CONTENTS

Ocean Acrobats

Lively bottlenose dolphins burst out of the ocean. With a splash, they dive back into the water. These ocean acrobats are **mammals**. They breathe air and give birth to live young.

Most bottlenose dolphins are about as long as a car. They are 9 to 12 feet (3 to 4 meters) long. They weigh about 500 pounds (227 kilograms).

mammal — a warm-blooded animal that has a backbone

dorsal fin →

flipper →

fluke

Built for Speed

A bottlenose dolphin's rocket-shaped body is built for speed. Their slippery skin cuts through the water. Powerful tail **flukes** move up and down like a paddle. They use flippers to steer. They use the **dorsal fin** on their backs to balance.

fluke — the wide, flat area of a dolphin's tail
dorsal fin — a fin that sticks up from a dolphin's back

Snouts, Teeth, and More

How did these dolphins get their name? Their **snouts** look like the neck of a bottle. Inside their mouths are almost 100 small, sharp teeth. Their teeth are perfect for catching slippery fish.

A blowhole helps a dolphin breathe. It opens at the water's surface. A strong skin flap covers the blowhole underwater.

snout — the long front part of a dolphin's head

Sound Effects

Dolphins also make sounds with their blowholes. The blowhole makes a sound like a balloon releasing air. A dolphin squeezes the blowhole opening to let out air. The air makes a squealing sound as it comes out.

blowhole

Life in the Sea

Bottlenose dolphins live in all the world's oceans. They live where the water is warm. Bottlenoses swim near Florida, Texas, and southern California.

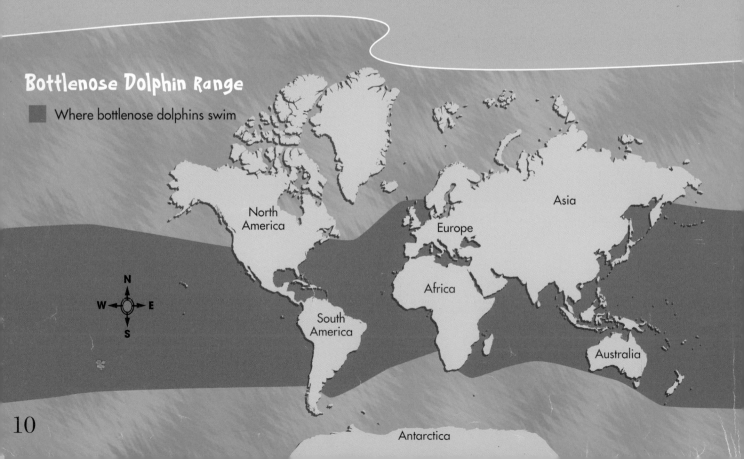

Bottlenose Dolphin Range

Where bottlenose dolphins swim

North America

Europe

Asia

Africa

South America

Australia

Antarctica

N
W E
S

Dolphins usually swim close to the ocean's surface. They also leap into the air. They can jump as high as 16 feet (5 meters). That's as tall as a giraffe!

Dinnertime!

Bottlenose dolphins eat almost any fish they can catch. They hunt in different ways. Sometimes dolphins surround a school of fish. Dolphins may also trap a school of fish near shore. But they can also dive very deep to find prey.

Dolphins grab fish with their sharp teeth. They swallow fish whole. Gulp!

Shades of Gray

Bottlenose dolphins' coloring helps them blend into the ocean. Dolphins' gray skin helps them sneak up on prey. It helps them hide from predators.

Catching Sound Waves

Dolphins use **echolocation** to find food. They make very high sounds from their blowhole area. The sound waves bounce off objects underwater. The sounds echo back to the dolphins. Sound waves tell the dolphins that there's something in the water.

echolocation — using sounds and echoes to find objects

Bottlenose Babies

Male and female bottlenose dolphins mate to produce young. After 12 months, one dolphin calf is born. Calves look like small adults. They are about 4 feet (1.2 meters) long. They have light lines on their bodies.

Calves are born ready to swim. They must get to the surface to take a breath. Sometimes they need a little push from their mothers.

Life Cycle of a Bottlenose Dolphin

Calf
Baby bottlenoses are about 4 feet (1.2 meters) long.

Young
Young bottlenose dolphins live with their mothers for about six years.

Adult
Adult male and female bottlenose dolphins rub noses before mating.

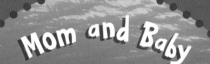

Mom and Baby

Better Together

Bottlenose dolphins live in groups.
Groups may be two to 15 dolphins.
Some groups have mothers and babies.
Other groups include only adult males.

Dolphins communicate with sounds, movements, and touches. Each dolphin has its own whistle. Through movement and sound, bottlenose dolphins make the ocean a lively place.

Amazing but True!

Some scientists believe bottlenose dolphins use sounds to stun prey. The dolphins make loud sounds that seem to make fish stop moving. The stunned fish are easier for dolphins to catch.

Bottlenose Dolphins and People

People enjoy watching bottlenose dolphins. These dolphins are smart and easy to train. But bottlenose dolphins also faced dangers from people. Years ago, dolphins were caught and killed in fishing nets. People polluted ocean waters. Today laws protect dolphins and make their ocean home safer.

Glossary

dorsal fin (DOR-suhl FIN) — the fin that sticks up from the middle of a dolphin's back

echolocation (eh-koh-loh-KAY-shuhn) — the process of using sounds and echoes to locate objects; whales and dolphins use echolocation to find food.

fluke (FLOOK) — the wide, flat area at the end of a dolphin's tail; dolphins move their flukes to swim.

mammal (MAM-uhl) — a warm-blooded animal that has a backbone

snout (SNOUT) — the long front part of an animal's head that includes the nose, mouth, and jaws

Read More

Ingram, Scott. *Dolphins.* Smart Animals! New York: Bearport, 2006.

Nicklin, Flip, and Linda Nicklin. *Face to Face with Dolphins.* Face to Face with Animals. Washington, D.C.: National Geographic, 2007.

Walker, Sally M. *Dolphins.* Nature Watch. Minneapolis: Lerner, 2008.

Internet Sites

FactHound offers a safe, fun way to find educator-approved Internet sites related to this book.

Here's what you do:

1. Visit *www.facthound.com*
2. Choose your grade level.
3. Begin your search.

This book's ID number is 9781429622646.

FactHound will fetch the best sites for you!

Index